this and that

a hodge podge of hülya's . . . poetry

hülya n. yılmaz

inner child press, ltd.

Credits

Author
hülya n. yılmaz

Foreword
Jackie Davis Allen

Editor
hülya n. yılmaz, Ph.D.

Cover Graphics & Design
William S. Peters Sr.
inner child press, ltd.

General Information
this and that
hülya n. yılmaz

1st Edition: 2019

This Publishing is protected under the Copyright Law as a "Collection". All rights for all submissions are retained by the individual author and or artist. No part of this publishing may be reproduced, transferred in any manner without the prior **WRITTEN CONSENT** of the "Material Owner" or its representative, Inner Child Press International. Any such violation infringes upon the Creative and Intellectual Property of the Owner pursuant to International and Federal Copyright Law. Any queries pertaining to this "Collection" should be addressed to the Publisher of Record.

Publisher Information: Inner Child Press International:
www.innerchildpress.com

This Collection is protected under U.S. and International Copyright Laws.

Copyright © 2019: hülya n. yılmaz

ISBN-13: 978-1-970020-70-0 (inner child press, ltd.)

$ 16.95

To the Poetry in You

Table of Contents

Proem   *xi*
Foreword   *xiii*

The Poetry

i still breathe	5
kissed by the wind	7
Daddy	8
may i play with you?	13
nature and i	14
oh, you precious little one!	15
what will it be?	18
oh, my sweet Daddy!	20
a yet-unborn poem	21
long after midnight	22
if "my" chipmunk could talk	24
my charming companions	26
Ahh, that Mediterranean Breeze!	27
Ma'rib	28
life is alive /	31
hayat yaşıyor /	31
das leben ist am leben	31
ignorance	32
routines	35
revolving doors	37
not a mere train ride	38
do the talk but also . . .	40

Table of Contents ... *continued*

self-entitled	41
when . . .	42
family	43
her pride	44
what i knew would simply not do!	46
lives wasted on the mundane	49
"Indian people are still here!"	51
is that what we call ours, ours?	53
impulsively /	57
dürtülü /	57
impulsiv	57
any questions?	58
"Once Upon a Time"	60
the colonialist	61
what else is left to do but . . .	62
nomads	63
a secret life-story	64
three, two, one	65
a daughter of Anatolia	66
even nature mourns /	69
doğa bile yas tutuyor /	69
sogar die natur trauert	69
like an eagle	70
Naren	72
Nimi'ipuu	76
jumping rope	78
our timeline knows	79
what a journey!	80
inventions, discoveries and donations	81

Table of Contents ... *continued*

the first snow /	85
ilk kar /	85
der erste schnee	85
no petting zoo	86
a coincidence?	89
where are you now?	93
in search of . . .	95
Pachacuti	97
if . . . /	99
Eğer ki . . . /	*99*
wenn . . .	*99*

A Special Place

lost . . . or?	103

Epilogue

about hülya n. yılmaz	109
What Others Are Saying . . .	113
hülya's Other Books	135
a few words from the Publisher	141

roem

As far back as I am able to remember, I have been inhibited. When the consent I gave to the intimate relationship between my pen and living at large was concerned. It has been a while since the last time my writings, life and I interacted in such a detached manner. I now write as life happens to me while I am being. Without inhibitions. So, I wrote *this and that* . . .

My hope is, dear reader, for my words in this book to resonate in your heart and mind long enough to allow room for a consideration of relevance in yours. Thank you for that effort.

hülya n. yılmaz

oreword

In 2014, I was invited to submit some of my poetry to *The Year of the Poet*, a monthly anthology of global endeavors. There, I discovered Hülya N. Yılmaz, Ph.D. I found her poetry mesmerizing. And, as a continuing member of that publication, since 2015, the poetry of Dr. Yılmaz has never failed to please. Acclaimed for her expertise as an editor for Inner Child Press International, she edited my two books. Her editing elevated my books to a level that sometimes surprised, but always pleased. I expect no less with my third book, *No Illusions, Through the Looking Glass*.

Hülya is multi-talented. And, as a poet in her own right, I am honored to have in my library, signed copies of her books, *Trance* and *Aflame*. Her poetry, in both books, as well as in *this and that*, is nothing short of amazing.

Inspired by memoir, most poems penned in English, some few others in German, as well as in her native tongue, Turkish, Hülya's poetry takes us on a journey. From the threads of her many travels, experiences and thoughts, she has masterfully woven the poetic fabric of *this and that*.

Dr. Yılmaz' poetry invokes the emotions which are common to all. However, it is how she has embroidered and infused them into the poetic fabric where we venture into her world. Reflecting the brilliance, with which only, she, as an accomplished, well-traveled writer is able to do, I invite you to settle back into a comfortable chair, and let Hülya's most recent collection of poetry, *this and that,* lead you into a realm of poetic beauty.

Jackie Davis Allen
Springfield, Virginia
12 November 2018

this and that

a hodge podge of hülya's . . . poetry

hülya n. yılmaz

The Poetry

hülya n. yılmaz

this and that

i still breathe

in the silence of the night
i breathe

and i devour everything the universe serves me
sipping each painful memory
the immense joys, before me
as my entree
magic keeps filling up my plate
sunshine-pouring centuries galore
intoxicating moments, in abundance

i am not void of vast sadness

for the dire persistence
of unspeakable acts
that nullify humanity
do not ever let me be
nor allow me to spread the wings
which were meant for me

my offerings are fragile in their built
for i carry too much guilt

my co-souls are dying
not of a gentle death

my co-spirits are suffering
not from nature's threat

but in the claws of a hungriest beast
against which i still do only the least
an act that does not suffice
to help anyone fly to glory
or to ease the pain so wide-spread
to ease it a little

at least by a tiny thread
of the man-made fate
oh, utterly gory

in the silence of the night
i breathe

just then
when i am about to soar into the sky
wrapped inside the gift of my serenity
my soul's eyes mirror an ear-piercing cry
in the silence of tears, frozen in mid-air to eternity
the agony of hearts, torn to non-count pieces
and then forced to ice, deep, to their core

i still breathe

all along, i know
for them, there just is
nowhere else to go
but into a blood-freezing abyss
of their doomed destiny
crafted by the cruelest of beasts
none other than the one
i continue to call
though in fact
it is not so at all:
the human species

i still breathe

oh, i breathe just fine

yet my breath
no longer feels divine

this and that

kissed by the wind

a butterfly came
for a visit just now
not long enough
for me to tell it a "hi"
a mere pit-stop
then, gone with the wind
it did not even stay
for the Turkish coffee on my tray

i wish i could prove its size to you
with a photo shoot in its prime
it was so tremendously big
that it would put a huge dent
on a fisherman's claim,
"i caught my biggest thus far!"

my butterfly was as enormous as
that intrusive eagle in the sky
honest! it was!

oh, my sweet butterfly
why did your wings take you up so high?

Daddy

in the tongue i learned from you and Mommy

kaç kere gördüm kendimi
o kaşığı ve çorba tasını tutarken titrek ellerimle
her seferinde senin beni
kah tam tanır kah başkasıyla karıştırır
ama o bana hep sevgiyle bakan
öpüp koklayan okşayan
senden aldığım renkteki
anlayış şefkat dolu gözlerin üzerimde
"Hülişim! Nasılsın kızım?"

hayatının belki de en zor o gününün akşamında
nasıl oldu da diyebildim ki ben sana
"Sakın gelme baba!
İnan, ikimiz de perişan oluruz sonra."

tamam sen hastaydın hem de epeyce
çoğumuzun ruhu duymuyorken
yaşlanmıştın çok hem de pek çok
her sevenimizin bildiği o keskin hafızan
artık değildi bize en yakın dün kadar

bana gelince . . .

tamam
kronik hastalığımdan edinmişim bir yoldaş
beni hiç bir zaman eski halime bırakmayacak

tamam
kendim ancak kendime yetebilen
ruhen bedenen madden

olsun!
ne olduysa olsun!

ne olursa olsun!

nasıl oldu da çıkabildi ağzımdan
o upuzun yoluna ta okyanus üzerinden
nankörlükle yoldaşlaşan
telefonumun o buz gibi ahizesine
sana doğru yola çıkan
o kalbimden silinesi kahrolası sözlerim?

senin nefesini duyabilen
iyice çökmüş ciğerlerinin
neredeyse üzerinde deri kalmamış
bedeninin üstündeki aciz iniş çıkışları gören
her bir hemşireye nasıl imrendim ah bir bilsen!
hele ki sana yemeğini verene
hem sana her gün bakarken hem de arkandan . . .

ne zihnim ne de kalbim
bana rahat nefes aldırmaz oldu
aldırmayacak da canım babam
hele ki ağabeyim senin o son resmini
bana gönderdiğinden beri

ölesiye üzgünüm hala Babacığım

beni affet ne olursun!
seni çok sevdim hep
hep seviyorum
seveceğim de hep
ne de olsa hala
senin her zamanki „Hüliş"inim ben
sana kendi son nefesine kadar minnettar
sana minikliğinden beri yolunu hiç şaşırmadan
hayran mı hayran „Hüliş"in

in the tongue of another

how many times have i imagined myself
holding that spoon and the soup-bowl
caressing your occasionally cognizant
but mostly unaware eyes
seeing in me someone else
your eyes that always glowed
with love, compassion, understanding,
and forgiving me, giving me hugs
in warmest soul-comforting kisses
those My Daddy-eyes
which gifted mine
with their hazel-color

"Hülişim! How are you, my girl?"

. . .

how could i possibly utter those words
in the night of your most-troubled day?

Don't come over, baba.
Believe me, we will
Both be miserable.

true

you were seriously ill

true

your mental you-ness
was declining so fast

true

this and that

your routinely sharp and expansive memory
famed among all our beloveds
was no longer intact
true

my by now-loyal for life-companion
that chronic physical dis-ease
would not even for a second
leave my side

true

i barely was enough
for my own self
psychologically
physically
financially

still!

how could i utter those cursed self-cursing
    curse-able words?
those damn-able haunting ungrateful words?
words that frivolously escaped my heart
and seeped through my iced-up receiver
on to their troubled self-troubling path
all the way over the ocean
to those My Daddy-eyes

. . .

i wish you knew, Babişim
how i envied then and after you passed
each one of your nurses who was there for you
who heard your faint yet still-breathing breaths
who saw how under your barely there-skin
your lungs still pumped their instinctive air faintly

hülya n. yılmaz

i covet still today
in times of my grave despair
that one particular nurse
the one who is busy beaming happily
while she is feeding you your soup

as the photograph of you
has related succinctly to me
the second to last photo that is
the one that my brother sent to me

neither my mind nor my heart
lets me take a guilt-free breath anymore

i am so sorry, canım Babam!
please forgive me!

i have always loved you

i love you today

i will love you every day

i am after all still your "Hüliş"
the one who has always been
your unwavering devoted admirer

i am in eternal gratitude for you
a fact that will never ever sway
even then when my last breath
is finally on its way

this and that

may i play with you?

a fox, bunnies
squirrels, chipmunks
wild birds of all walks of life
i welcome without the least of a strife
spiders however . . .
oh no oh my no chance!
they just got to go
and not a mere to and fro
do they really think
i would ever give in?
oh no oh my no chance!
okay okay . . .
it was my fault
i was in a trance
still . . . they'd better know
none of them is welcomed here

while the others stay at a respectful distance
one of these my-fobia-subject crawlers
(oh my so very creepy!)
takes its liberty
way over the limit
of my endless tolerance

i am passionate about gun control, mind you
but hey, if this one keeps it up like this
i won't blink a second, and believe me
i won't miss
i will shoot it to death
right in each of its eerie legs

. . .

Ahh, what a bliss!

nature and i

leaves were raining this morning
and now the rain covets them eagerly

glued to my comfortable chair
under the sky-copy-catting blue
of my patio's umbrella
inhaling nature's playfulness

not one soul in sight but i

my four-legged buddies?
who knows where they are!

i am busy devouring myself
here and in the now

oh, you precious little one!

with gorgeous hope-eyes

which of them was robbed from you
ever so abruptly, cruelly
in blood-chilling monstrosities?

was it your mother or your father?

maybe both . . .

you are in hunger pains, i know
and as thirsty as those war mongers' obsession to slay
yet, so helpless as they never seem to be

my entire being craves
to cradle you inside my body
back to your somewhat-safe times
i am already singing you a lullaby
hoping to lead you to a sedating sleep
to send you back to your dreams of innocence
so much so that they become a reality for you

a few seconds ago, i have eagerly fetched
my for too long-dried-out mother's milk
in abundance, it will pour out for you
for i have committedly willed it so
i want it to nourish your tiny half-cut frame
together with the shards of your little heart
that was ever-so-brutally smashed
an uncut diamond, that is what you are
shattered before you were even born

your wingless soul also came to me
she too is invited to our feast

as for your angel-spirit
she was meant to fly up high

so, i let her free
and, she now soars
above and beyond the sky
tucked in somewhat safely

please, don't you crawl away in a rush
i do not want you to go there
not yet anyway

. . .

i have been repeatedly told
that i am good at make-believe

you can tell me how my dreaming fared
when you and i once again have it made

. . .

a life of marvels awaits your path's stretch
don't you ever mind the killers' vulgar stench!

when compared with how they reek
(though thinking so is insane!)
the scent our dead begin to ooze
will make utterly envious
Sweet Pea's newest blooms

sleep, my nameless little angel!
sleep as angelically as only you can do!

my all-loving heart
and my resolute mind
will learn how to suitably soothe

this and that

my unstoppable-y wailing soul
so that my mother-hands will knit
your receiving-blanket into a shield
invisible to the sadistic beast
which calls itself *human*
but is not one in the least

i will lay myself down next to you
i promise you, i will not leave . . .

not before you let go of your last breath
you shall at least not face the fangs of death
in the cruel, bloody hands of Man's vomited filth

sleep, Mother Earth's untainted scream!
forgive me in your purest dream
for all the deeds i could have done
but in passionate paralysis
i repeatedly failed to do
forgive me in your innocence
for all the miracles you had hoped
that i could capably proclaim
but in emotive weakness
i repeatedly failed to do

. . .

all that is anon left in me
that is due to you, for you
is the might in my strength
to caress you deep in my soul
until, for eternity, on to your wasted
trail of love you go

what will it be?

the night is snowing into the sky
where it clears up the tracks, left over
from unforgettable sad memories of the past
apprehensions, doubts and fears of the new
intertwine persistently in a binding chain
and trace me back to times long-passed
of those countless, my uncertain days

you had once told me
i would tiptoe through the garden
of my window

i chose to dance
on the fragile glass
of its outright narrow sills

and . . .

although the ground
was not too far to fall upon
the thought of a head-on crash
had been a concern at my age
no worries, was the invite
which i desired to embrace

and . . .

i have
readily
willingly

everything progressed so fast
initially, steadily, cherish-ably

this and that

there continues to be a worry
deep enough at the core of me
it is the silence
you have bathed me with since
that which to me is a big mystery

it is not without respect
that i try to understand at my best

but . . .

time is not patient in waiting
it is adamant and keeps nagging
making me think, then over-think

what will it be?

hülya n. yılmaz

oh, my sweet Daddy!

you were on foreign soil
Mom chose not to hurt you while there
then, the day of your scheduled arrival came
and i saw your soul's sorrow put mine to shame

i still see you in my heart's eyes
through the parents-room, left ajar
how hard you cried, sobbing all along
what i thought to have lasted for too long

Dad, i now know more than ever before
what it means for a fortress to be gone
i, too, find myself in a forsaken desert
with no hope for an oasis to come

a yet-unborn poem

i was just about to open
    the curtain of the window
        next to my patio –my sanctuary
            when I saw one bird
                on the closest bird-feeder.
                    i stopped to eavesdrop.
that beautiful being
    was eagerly shuffling
        the seeds without eating any.
            i have been curious
                about the behavioral patterns
                    of these little avians before.
this one was strategically
    dropping the seeds to the ground.
        another bird of the same kind
            cautiously perched
                on the now-delicatessen-filled
                lawn below,
                    waiting to be fed. i took my time
                      with my morning-flow.
the Sun, the mid-summer breeze
    and the crisply dawning-air
        waited without a complaint
            for the dining couple's ritual to end.
                i no longer had any reason to despair.

long after midnight

the moon has been playing with me
for the last couple of nights
showing off one minute overtly
hiding behind clouds in the next

i am being overly anxious perhaps
in my passionate want to indulge
in its sweet enticing quintessence

could my pure infatuation
have turned into a nuisance
not to forget my mere presence?

to offer it my awe and admiration
to let it feel my love and my passion
is all that i had innocently intended

in my childlike girlish desperation
i had merely wished to become
its exclusively betrothed

could such intent have transpired
as something utterly threatening
although it had come to me first
and enchanted me with its shine?

am i in fact one of the others?

should i have taken smaller steps?

if only i had not gotten to it this close!

this and that

i wish i had the courage to compose
this entire thing in a letter as prose
i joyfully would have signed it then
anonymously wholly eternally yours

if "my" chipmunk could talk

flowers . . .
in a bouquet of colors
rain-showered freshly

indoor plants . . .
showing of their well-earned drops of sweat
in their temporary home, the wild wild wild indoors

one bird-seed-tower . . .
a multi-flat avian-condo
emptied before it can dangle on its shepherd hook

the other feeder . . .
a villa compared to its safely-distanced neighbor
ready to cater a larger-than-ever-squirrel convention

a chipmunk . . .
busy re-arranging the patio furniture
shooting out disapproving glances at its version before

a broken ground-light . . .
waiting to be glued to health
having refused the Gorilla Glue as its mate

the non-smoker-worthy ashtray . . .
cuddled up with a Citronella bucket
enchanted by the lure of a cozy tryst

last year's garden art . . .
each piece as vibrant as it was then
a little worn-out in their eye-catching sheen

this and that

the old loyal Bistro set . . .
trapped in its primal space
vying for one more breath

taking on a growingly greener tint
blatantly shamelessly in plain sight
right before the rebuking eyes of this summer's seats

blah blah blah . . .

enough already!
all is cool and dandy
but i need a big bowl of candy
unless she moves out and abound
my sweets cannot eat chat or frolic around
hungrier by each wasted second is my family
this woman is surely an anomaly!
she'd better hand over fast
the cotton-tailed bunny to me at last
if she refuses to comply
i will forever be her archenemy

my charming companions

After all those overjoyed visits, i had
concluded we would be there
for one another for life

Alas! We are no longer!

Having sensed my persistent longing, bunnies
now keep me company at each night
so long as i sit out here eyeing them from a distance
so long as i control my overzealous mothering act

of wanting to constantly feed them

If i lose my composure, i
suspect, they too will leave me behind

Yet, all along
i had assumed
my cooking skills were
sufficient to say the least

i have learned my lesson . . .

i no longer indulge myself in lending any of them
my well-intended, acutely attentive, high-demand attention
i will be, pronto, mindful to mindfully let them self-engage
in their long-cherished
allow me-to be myself-geared-life instead

as for me . . .
i will try to just be
as they ever so brilliantly
appear to want to be

this and that

Ahh, that Mediterranean Breeze!

a warm soft breeze became my wrap today
i deeply inhaled my sweet Mediterranean's air
that deep breath's former ground-shaking effect
no longer amazed me, i found, in its diligent reach
it could not arrive at the depths of my deepest depth

once again, you came for a brief visit last night
and your old vision lingered on and on in my mind
because i opted to choose to allow it
to warmly surround me

oh no!
i did not cry this time
i guess i had invited you in
wanting to thank you once more
to share with your spirit my utter gratitude

even when i hit many a bottomless pit back then
i have always been eternally grateful to you
it is now a clearer realization though
how fulfilled i was in my appreciation
for all the gifts you have adorned me with
for all the heart's sufferings you had poured
into the essence of my often-too fragile being
for all that everything we were for each other once

Be well, dear heart! Be very well!
Always and forevermore

Ma'rib

i time-travel frequently
to far-away places and times

Do not misunderstand!

It is thus not because i am incapable to cope
with where i am when i am who i am. It is
simply so by choice. We all have
that explosive button
at our fingertips.
Do we not?

This time, i left
for Ma'rib to partake
of its much-anticipated fall.

Wait, wait, disregard that!
i have to self-correct:
to witness for a little while
a bit its oft-quoted glory.

It was the years between?

Hmm . . .

At any rate, it surely was
many a century, even moons ago.
Let us estimate the time-frame to be
within the perimeters of
the 8th century BC
and the 5th of AD.

What matters is the fact
that i have indeed come back
to tell you wholeheartedly a tiny story

this and that

all the way from an era of notable glory.

Take a look!

What you see on the sand of the Ma'ribian desert,
deep down at the bottom of their incredible Dam,
are my footprints, firmly marked forever on each.

Those fine particles between my toes
made an out-of-this-world promise to me:
they will never give my ignorance away . . .
If, that is, i honored my initial intent to stay,
to which i replied in my heart's tongue:
my spirit could not abandon you ever!
For, you see, i had begun to fiercely shiver
in an ecstasy so prolifically profound
that i could not help but to compare
the touch of their incitingly hot stare
to my beloved King Solomon's affair
with Sheba, his Queen, totally bare soul-wise,
legendarily beautiful and well-dressed otherwise;
so much so that i had been admiring both of them since
from afar of their long-ago times, from their there, but
just here, where i am now and have always been.

But then . . .

resurfaced, flooding along
their insatiable hunger for the sacrifice of the innocent
the cold-blooded powers-to-be.

To my eternally aflame despair,
my time capsule rushed to bring me back.

My ignorant grown-up-eyes did, after all, lack
the growingly-notorious record of the eternal love
that my own era cherished for the affairs of the dark.

Perhaps, just perhaps
you would care to join me

in my time capsule. In it, there are
reserved seats for many.

this and that

life is alive

heavy rain poured down
roads joined in the rascals' fun
a rainbow peeked through

hayat yaşıyor

yağmur şiddetle indi
sokaklar bu muzurun eğlentisinde
doğdu bir gök kuşağı

das leben ist am leben

heftig fiel zum boden der regen
die strassen machten den schlingelspass mit
da kam zur welt ein regenbogen

ignorance

a woman of Turkish birth
who in other words should know better
having been born into the same region and religion
having received, though with some interruption
her early, mid-level and high school education
in an equally Islamic country
regardless of any variation

after settling in North America
coming to terms with Islam, its women and men
within the pre-scribed rigid boundaries of her schooling
she determinedly sought the highest possible form of
    education
for her own sake, to the point to be able to expose
    unilaterally
all that which aims to confine the female territory
in their public sphere but also in that of their privacy

years passed
in fact, decades were gone

her lifelong passion for poetry
accompanied her to the Middle East
Jordan was the first stop-nation on her route
a festival of festivals took her to the city of Jerash
the amazingly intact, world's awe Roman Amphitheater
offered to the first night of poems a fairy-tale-like home
poets from across the globe joined in the shared breathing
of the magically fresh air for the furthering of their
    inspiration

this and that

a gloriously triumphant, one-of-a-kind celebration
    took place
this timeless art surpassed any and all potential limitation
    of space
it gracefully accompanied the mesmerizing dance steps
    of the old
a breathtakingly melodic language introduced
    the many verses
in a soothingly gentle, sweetest and an intoxicating
    embrace
a rarest form of a jubilant friendship swayed in mid-air
and dashed about, hand in hand, with mutual wonder
patting the poets' ink into a forthright admiration

the same ignorant female
inhaled every precious hug in a child's utter awe
throughout the following festival days and nights
contemplating all along, how she could live without . . .

Al-Karak was for some poets the last stop
the regal beauty of the valleys and the mountains
along the way to the Castle of histories, long passed
astonished her out of her ignorance of the past
the Domed Stable from the Ottoman Era
graciously welcomed the visibly inspired souls
more poems attained their momentarily-lasting fame
as continuous readings met a vigorous applause

her breath was taken away
as unconditional love for the poetic art
and for each with a passion to compose it
filled the air in eager and plentiful abundance

there stood a preciously tender plate of a kind of affection
she had never expected, or could have imagined
    to live before

under her hat as the former ignorant witness . . .

thus, she dove
peacefully into love
and divine acceptance

this and that

routines

i wake up to just another day
and am soon on my way to work
a school bus waits at the curbside
its hugs, ready for the bubbly children
anxious parents, in orderly lines, are also there
to see their babies off to their safety-ridden returns

i think back and reminisce in peace
about my own child's schooling ease

. . .

children get born also
in other parts of our world, of course!
children are cherished also
in other parts of our world, of course!
children are loved also
in other parts of our world, of course!

some, having to struggle to stay alive
some, only allowed the choice to try
for death manages to find them
when they are way too young

too many are too often left behind
without a guardian's devoted, caring love
and so, for the rest of their butchered lives
they end up awaiting their pre-determined fate

the notoriously grim age-old reaper, after all,
has for long committed itself to a lethal contract:
to annihilate, together with all infamous psychopaths
from in- and outside those precious little beings'
unfortunate, doomed-at all cost-nations of birth

in those long-forgotten geographies
a school bus might, indeed, succeed
in a repeat-rewind-repeat-appearance
probably, in a so-called "neutral zone"
or in a "no-dispute area", for instance

such an outcome would, for sure, be a rare sight
maybe even enough to make the evening news
with a self-indulging, self-approbated pride
but any soul-empty headline will be short-lived
just like the precious little ones that were inside
for, the moment the bus doors begin to open wide
that supposedly-safe, supposedly-routine daily ride
will start spitting out tiny corpses, bones on the side

this and that

revolving doors

door #1

you sound different
not like your usual self
confused, sad, in despair?

then comes your desperate plea

i hear it but choose to flee

i've decided, my girl
i'm coming to stay with you

        how could i be so indifferent!

                door #2

            i see through the mundane
        i not only hear but i also listen
      i sense something is just not right
     i can almost touch and feel your plight

               of course, Dad!

not a mere train ride

sitting in the train to Alexandria
a considerable distance from her,
Turkey, that is, my country of birth
a flood of Egyptians rushing back and forth
some are still attentive to our "we are lost"-looks
and try to help us out, all the way to our compartment

cool air
so refreshing

comfortable seats

the over-head space, generously accommodating
like the hand-picked goodies in our meal-boxes
our hotel's cook prepared each of them for us
at the crack of dawn, not aghast at our alarm

i try to hear and see all that is around me
what prevails is one singular memory
that of another station for trains
Ankara's main *Tren Garı*

on time, the four of us had gathered there
as my mind now travels to that long-ago past
we stood by the platform to Istanbul to see you off

your first-time-ever absence
from our unity as a family

on our somber ride back home, Dad told us
you had left for a visit with your best friend
i still don't know as to why she needed you so

this and that

if my no-longer-as-diligent brain activity is right
my tears were racing down my face in all their might

life suddenly had no taste, no meaning anymore
Mom, i was missing you terribly at my core

nothing has changed, in actuality
unlike you, i am close to making it to 63
i miss you more and more by each passing day
for much longer, Dad, thankfully, willed to stay
i am utterly grateful for his healthy 90+ years
which the Universe graced us with no fears
no matter who says to me what
his passing remains a deepest cut
inside each of the chambers of my heart

my middle name should not have been Naciye
for i know myself best in my ill-famed naivete
what on earth could i have been thinking
when i, those many moons ago,
dared to believe that the two of you
would be living happily forevermore

a mere train ride this is to many
a basic move from point A to point B
to me, however, it has an ineffable lure
for it has just managed to bring back
my overwhelming memories of yore

hülya n. yılmaz

do the talk but also . . .

"in the blink of an eye," we say

"everything can end"

clear, or as in a blend

images run amok, with no intent to stay

survivors, indeed, do the talk

as i did and continue to do

but i am beyond grateful

for i also walk the walk

self-entitled

Kudos to the British!

They worked also the 19th century
to their best possible advantage as
they managed to take home the bounty
yet once again ever so deviously.

The poor unknowing Spanish!

A rushed glimpse of the Tuvalu islands at least
discouraged them from continuing to feed on
their insatiably power-hungry ruling beast

Alas!

Though they failed their quest to fully discover
the land's incredible richness in phosphate, they
made sure to arrange for it to be mined by the islanders.

All profits were fed-exed to the Commonwealth's plate.

when . . .

on my way home from a long day's work
i stop myself on my routinely safe old track
i pause to feel, in fact, to let the bitter cold seep
first through the daringly exposed pores of my skin
then to a freeze that is ever-so-unsettlingly deep
all along, i think: what is it that i lack?

while i gleefully type these lines on my phone
my freezing fingers let out a sound-rich groan
the gloveless hand begins a desperate plea
from the biting cold, it wants to cowardly flee
its too familiar, warmth-gifting, knitted shield
does not seem to be an embraceable sacrifice
it, at any time soon, would be willing to wield

when i start to lose the feel of my favorite big toe
i, too, am no longer eager or able to play the hero
besides, my limbs' voiced complaints keep rising
i will not, nor do i have to, face a futile uprising
so, in less than a dizzying one single minute's time
i am inside my car, praising comfort's warm chime

driving back to unite with my home's convenience
i realize, i am only willing to offer little to none lenience
when it comes to my own input in all the outside-me-affairs
whatever pushes to stir up my comfort about others' flares
has no chance with me, their reach is out of the-way
i have no room for them even for a one-night stay

this and that

family

love was the guest of honor
it outshone the sun's high-summer rays
the smile of each soul was lit by an embrace
and delivered to me tenderly with utter grace

> my blood family had passed away
> long ago, without a trace

> how clueless of me!

> i used to think that irreplaceable gift
> had abandoned me once and for all
> yet, it has been by my side all along
> at those times, when i rejoiced
> and whenever it was that i have mourned

love was the guest of honor
it outshone the sun's high-summer rays
the smile of each soul was lit by an embrace
and delivered to me tenderly with utter grace

> i thus embarked on
> an incredible journey
> amid the precious members
> of my beloved's family

love was the guest of honor
it outshone the sun's high-summer rays
the smile of each soul was lit by an embrace
and delivered to me tenderly with utter grace

her pride

the train to Alexandria has come a long way

i leave "First Class" to smoke
a young woman is sitting on the floor
her toddler just lies there, between her legs
atop her multiple-layered outer dress

she offers me a bag
one of the many of her hauling
so that my cigarette and i
would be seated comfortably

i thank her in what i know in her tongue
Şükran –Thank You and finger-point my heart
as a sign of "no need", following a few nicotine inhales

she gently touches my leg this time
now, she has spread an unused bag for me
right beside her and her still unmoving child

i sit down by her
while i signal eagerly
my clumsy *Şükran* once more

her precious little one seems to be asleep
he (she?) stirs a bit but goes back to a slumber, quite deep
on his (her) tiny hand, an IV piece, with its tape fully intact
no hair in his (her) exposed, limp-all-around body
though i fear that it will be a violation of her privacy
i unveil my urge to feel the life of her fragile birth-gift
she sweetly signals me back that she would not mind
encouraged, i reach to his (her) arms, legs
he (she) does not move

in an obvious despair
but still holding on to hope
his (her) mother's prayer-eyes meet mine
in our tongue-tied tears, we then unite

thankful, for she has allowed me
into her utterly private sphere,
i touch her young, beautiful face
and we join in a whisper at once:

İnşaallah! – May Allah Be Willing!

what i knew would simply not do!

Ethiopia
of the early Christian era
but, a Red Sea ruler?

. . .

empires surely rise
and, as we live it
every day today,
they also fall

out of history's authentic tracks, that is

white men get to etch in stone make-believe memories
in acid, for ages, on the indestructible fabric of lies to come
together, of course, with eager co-travelers – their women
who, in the footsteps of their 19th century
Orientalist counterparts, first became enchanted
by the exotic object of their own lush fantasies
but then also upon their return to their home countries
those whites, in unison, opted to adhere themselves
in a perfectly-mastered, selfish sense of loyalty
to the paintings, writings or the chanting of pieces
of mesmerizing, though largely imaginative, stories
all of which continue today to serve to totally dominate
in the thrones of their self-appointed subject – *the Self*
of only their own highest, self-serving esteem
in its collectively manipulative existence

the "Other" is eternally doomed
in fact, it was always thus doomed
doomed beyond any potential
for any corrective markings
on any of the related texts
doomed far, far beneath

this and that

the abyss of eternity
so, history's white books of highly-selective-memory
indoctrinate, over and over, as our times evidence clearly
they rob everyone else from mounting the other self justly
those powers of self-erected "superior" thrones
write and write and write in their self-designated
cannot live without-we are superior-importance
for clueless generations, with no end to come
they overwhelmingly mark down their worth
on self-constructed, indestructible paper, which
is reserved for a reading by their sheeple-masses
no matter how quickly their chairs' life-capacity
outgrows their miniscule acts of competence
they, time and again, completely fail everyone else
for they have only room for their incurable ignorance

. . .

The Aksum Kingdom, too, was doomed
doomed to remain as "the inferior other"
lest it be revered for what it had in fact been:
a domain of many a notable accomplishment
among our present world's eminent civilizations
worthy of noble representations
and pride-filled re-presentations

it, instead, was doomed

if only this empire had not yielded to an act of discovery
as a black-achievement in its disturbing bottom line-reality!

if only this empire had not been created
as a "promised land for uprooted Africans"

if only this empire had not been revived
within its world-awing, powerful existence
under the painstaking efforts of the enslaved

18th-century black preachers in an undying presence

as for the good ol' United States . . .

what will be your service to history?

Aksum's origin is, after all
not something to be traced back
to the kingdoms of the Semitic alone . . .

this and that

lives wasted on the mundane

please do not tell me anymore
how to cross my sitting-legs in a skirt
to hide well under my pants that private fabric
in what age order to serve guests Turkish coffee
what not to do with the table crumbs
(no sweeping into that willing groove of my hand!)
not to laugh heartily in public
to wait for my turn in speaking up anywhere

my instincts never had any trouble
accommodating the most obvious
catering to the needs and wants
of every one, just not my own
while i knew each of you
were only meaning well
while you cradled me
through a life of love

. . .

i am of old age now
and i have had enough!

still doing no harm to anyone
with not even an ounce of ill-will
in any of my genetically-sound cells
or inside the chambers of my purest heart

i am as gentle as ever before
even toward all of those souls
who have no business in mine

i had my share of personal sacrifices
for many a decade and then some . . .

i am of old age now
and i have had enough!

please do not judge me anymore
for acts that i have not undertaken
or for those i am happy to commit
with no inhibitions
no hesitations
through love
with love
in love
love for one
and love for all

a few more chunks of life are awaiting me
i find out these days in pure delight

i continue to care about you for you
though only then when i am allowed
regardless, i do so behind closed doors
caringly, tirelessly and with all my might

so, won't you, please, try a bit at least
not to turn my utter joy and true happiness
into a wasted-time or a purely mundane plight?

this and that

"Indian people are still here!"

Otis Halfmoon of the Nez Percè tribe maintains:

"We are not going away. It is time
That the newcomers to this country
Start paying proper respect
To the elder status
Of the first nations."

Chief Joseph adds:

"Every animal knows more than you do.
White men have too many chiefs.
Learn how to talk. Then learn how to teach."

a nation
whose population marked
its commitment to live in peace
yet was forced to dress in war-wear
simply because the government of the U.S.
began to shoo it away, way down below and
underground, into the so-called safe reservations

in the words of the reservation doctor
he died of a broken heart
his countless appeals
to federal authorities
hit, after all,
a deaf wall

"I am tired of fighting . . . from where
The sun now stands. I will fight no more",
uttered In-mut-too-yah-lat-lat.

Chief Joseph, once again, did not mince his words:

"Thunder coming up over the land from the water."
He, Chief Joseph as he now is known to us
spoke up with passion and persistence
about the proudly ignorant populace
that which eroded more of his land

one night after another
one dark night at a time

one day after another
one darker day at a time

. . .

let us pay homage
and recall the times
when we have all died
a death by a broken heart

this and that

is that what we call ours, ours?

my life in Turkey was multi-colored
brown and dark brown were the most favorite hues
served inside delicately-painted, frailly, little cups
they were devoured by the dearest indulging
who passed the age-limit with flying collars

thanks to a multitude of gatherings
i watched joyfully time and time again
many a rite of that simple true pleasure
and observed how my ancestors consumed
the thick strong- and bitter-looking taste
sweetened only by a delicious mix
of laughter-typhoons and mouth-watering
gentlest, lullaby-like, mesmerizing-ly gorgeous
collective-art of masterful story-telling

often, a jamboree of exotically aromatic spices
materialized right before my eyes
and all the senses of the dearly-gathered
while they, sip by sip, went on to starvingly inhale
the short-lived though lastingly multi-tiered hot vapor
that oozed from the heavy syrup-attired,
ready-for a new paint-walls
of our little but heart-heated home
all the way to my behind-the-doors dancing steps
then into my heart's vast collection of inestimable memories

Turkish coffee . . .

Ahh!

soon after i graduated
to my loved ones' passable grade in age
i accumulated an army of those intricately
hand-made ceramic art pieces . . . one sip by one sip

not even the slightest trace was ever left behind . . .
of the dark matter that once belonged to their insides

worse!

i started to call them "mine"

resorting, with no waste of a millisecond, to the
olden, seemingly-plausible lessons of time
in my own defense; choosing to heed
my learned inner-voice:
Turkish coffee has always been
solely in the custody of the Turks

besides . . .

everyone in my immediately familiar
but also, distantly-tied vicinities knew
how it, long ago, was baptized as "ours"
having held on to its supreme reign
for countless memorable years
so powerfully controlled that
the entire world
still speaks
of it today!

then . . .

i became
an older grown-up
and re-conceptualized:
what if that knock-out flavor
that offered itself to us to savor
along with its magically-aromatic spices
were never ours to begin with, to claim as "ours"
but was rather invented and even toiled over
by civilizations of the long-ago forgotten past

this and that

not unlike the one of the Sabaeans, for instance
whose Ma'rib, the hub-city of their regime's
mid-century-epoch, claimed to have earned
its due-fame for its spectacular temples
disaster-resistant monuments but also
for its undeniably state-of-the-art
agricultural prosperity

. . .

Turkish coffee?
Turkish spices
with the know-how to enhance
that unique brew's perception?

what if

its creation
had nothing to do
with Turkish-ness?

what if

its construct
was rooted, let's say
in Sabaean ancestry?

what if

. . .

what if
we just stopped to care
about things so mundane
and would re-learn instead
our gifted one-and-only destiny
thus, allow it to be immortally re-born

as the integral element of our original self
which many moons ago was the sole stronghold
of that which we, the people
of the so-called "modern" times
ever so dismissively
insensitively
ignorantly
dare to label as "humanity"

impulsively

senseless are the tears
if ice-cold the many souls
humanity sleeps

dürtülü

anlamsızdır gözyaşları
bunca buza dönmüş ruh karşısında
insanlık derin bir uykuda

impulsiv

sinnlos die tränen
wenn eiskalt viele seelen
die menschheit schläft tief

any questions?

tens of vultures huddled
playing phone tag
with those in the farthest distance

they all must have heard it by now

breathing bodies lain there to feast on
tiny, unprotected, not-yet-knowing-how to-walk bodies
with each of their soon-to be-bloodied cells cringing
their half-closed, fear-laden eyes searching
for their mommies and daddies
while their fading whispers
hold on to their last hope

other adults would come

and when they do

the babies' hurts will be no longer
first will come a warm, calming hug
"everything will be okay"-kind of a-hug
then, their aching tummies will be sated
while they will be warmly wrapped
inside a receiving blanket of love
they will soon fall into a sweet slumber
which will bring back their mommies and daddies
into their yet-untainted dreams

. . .

not quite!
not even close!
oh no!

get ready, you dearest little souls

this and that

too many grown-ups want you to die
but before you pass on to the yonder
which they themselves dread to death
throughout their miserable lives
know that there is plenty of them creating havoc
sick, in violent delight, they run out and about
and opt to play hide-and-seek all around

they come in different shapes and sizes

they have, however, one gene in common:
their heart slithers under the same reptiles' rock

so, they all don in their rotting unified-inside
a post-birth malfunction that is one of a kind

"Once Upon a Time"

there was an island called "Nauru"
1,400 people lived on it in peace
they spoke their native tongue
they had their native culture
phosphate, in abundance

the year was 1843 then

45 years later
only 900 survived
together with their phosphate

what about their language
what about their culture, you ask?

into yet another abyss they went

this and that

the colonialist

does the name "Cook", James Cook
as in Captain James Cook, that is
sound familiar to you

no, you say?

how can that be!

he has a monument in his name, you see
for the monumental service he has done in 1774
he proudly did vandalize, torture, butcher and colonize
the intact-natives of Vanuatu Islands of the year 500 BCE
he whitened them ever so graciously
with his own label:
The New Hebrides

you get it, of course

there was nothing "new" about the host-land
until that kill-all year ambushed it mercilessly

then

they were no more
the same as they were before

the white legacy!

isn't it just grand?

what else is left to do but . . .

to bow in highest respect
before the pens of one such power
that even supersedes
the brutality of the
segregationist
colonialist
chauvinist
ethnicist
sexist
racist
one that surpasses time and space
as only the unwavering ink can do

now is the only time
and here, the only place
where we must and shall
unconditionally embrace

for one single loss from our unity in diversity
is a cause for an irreversible tragedy
that will appoint us with no delay
to the expiry of our humanity

nomads

"very little is known about their lives",
is the professional claim of our times

our times' supposedly-modern jest
won't be as terse about us, i suspect
we have, after all, a dire need
to self-glorify in retrospect

i don't want to doubt what is said about you today
whenever i look at our conditions in dismay
the continent you discovered among the first
then managed to peacefully inhabitate
is yelped to be the solely greatest
but just when i think i mastered
the darning of the nth rave
then comes the latest

your surviving ancestors may 9,000 years later
discover or make for us, a laughing stock, a grater
for we yearn for the ultimate fine-tuning of all times
our predicament must, at all cost, unveil its fatal secret
maybe then one can distill this pickle, oh so terribly acrid!

you were a wandering and gathering lot, i heard
we, on the other hand, are an incessantly scattering herd
you clothed yourselves with the skin of your difficult hunt
and eaten plants to stay alive, while we go the other way
and lust after nature which soon will meet its doomsday

a secret life-story

seriously!

it's impossible for our live-records to stay unknown
even long after our skeletons' offspring has outgrown
their offspring's sketches that map the ruins of the land
there will always be a soul to give our grim tale a hand

has it not been so through the timeline of humanity?
when will we begin to see this nightmare in all clarity?
what does it take to note all the accomplished wrongs?
why look so far while they parade right here in throngs?

seriously!

what kind of a delete-button did in your testimonies?
you surely had a bunch of rationally honest cronies
it just cannot be that so little of you was left behind!
was perchance the mass of your bands prenatally twined?

you were, after all, the inhabitants of Southwest-U.S.A.
and of Mexico in the North, well-synchronized, i daresay
to all that which you achieved in 10,000 or 40,000 years
some of us rashly succumb, simply to forsake our tears

this and that

three, two, one

they faded away
in the mist above the mountains
little black birds in the number of three
as small as my own i lately appears to me

did they go over there
where my near-sighted past aimed to be
or are they right here, near, yet much farther away?

at the old horizon's distance, anew
where my mind dares to stay today
a desperately-imagined door is left ajar
in the vastness of the land and its incredible sky

little black birds in the number of three
each as small as i most certainly am to me
as small as each of us truly is in reality
despite our self-celebrating exclusivity

there, in fact, is only one enormous entity
that sees through our pitifully miniscule stature
it notes its vacuity against its own eternal grandeur
and pities its inability to spread on now or henceforth

the unfathomable expanse of the universe . . .

three little birds
two little birds
one little bird

a daughter of Anatolia

home to fertile civilizations for years
in multiplied thousands

a grandiose spread of bountiful nature
her integral riches, a modest splendor
distinct collections of artifacts

Ottoman Empire is on its way to fade away

with the onset of the year 1923
a multitude of reforms are set free
a republic is born

neither the Europeans of the West
nor the cultures of the Near East
are any contest to it
as far as civilized neweties

Mustafa Kemal's Turkey
learns women's rights

public seclusion of women is no more
females proudly trot on public sphere
doctors
lawyers
educators
parliamentarians
open-platform speakers
writers in fact a notable number of writers

the infant republic
meets her first president
the world-renowned Atatürk

this and that

a visionary
a rights-fighter
the gentle father of Anatolia

she leads a prosperous life
is envied by the aggressive back then-world-powers
and abundantly spreads to and through all her territories

the immediate and cosmic success
of the historically marked miraculous come-back
from the ruins of a longest-lived empire
the once-self-celebrated Ottoman spheres
recover from their prolonged death-bed-occupancy

women are liberated
the women of Anatolia

countless daughters merge
from their secluded observation towers
and take their rightful place as cultural icons

immersed in a cycle of an all-inclusive diversity,
faiths of all walks of life settle in safely inside her
while they don a dance of joy
in honor of her legacy

co-existence rules

decades pass

Anatolia hears a knock on her door

corruption
disruption
destruction
deconstruction
religion's unreligious re-construction

barge in along with their brain-washed populace

her entryway
which for decades
forbade all darkness
is suddenly plundered

the masterfully orchestrated brutal kicks
deliberately vicious strikes for a full-blown ruin
have their way of raping her away

a tyrant violates mercilessly
Anatolia and her daughters
"for the sake of Turkey's progress,"
is the disguise he and his loyal beasts

hide behind cowardly and relentlessly
while they eradicate her glorious inborn gifts
inhumanity and an all-consuming Stone-Age mentality
rule over the once-untouchable beauty of Anatolia today
implanting into her womb eternally-barren ovaries
her promised fate is no more
furthermore, this despot and his herd
leave no room for a single drop of hope
for her daughters' off-springs
to remain intact beyond this date

this and that

even nature mourns

clouds tear up sighing
children no longer playful
what did we create

doğa bile yas tutuyor

bulutların bile iç çekerken gözleri bulutlanıyor
artık oyunlar uzak çocuklardan
ne yaptık biz böyle

sogar die natur trauert

seufzend überwältigen tränen die wolken
kinder sind nicht mehr spiellustig
was haben wir bloss erstellt

like an eagle

İstanbul dons a large number of majestic forts

Those structures from many ancient histories
May today not appear as powerful anymore
But the debris alone suffice to astound
The willing eye through a mere peek
At the hauntingly mighty Bosphorus
In sync with the influential breaths
That many civilizations of the past
Have generously left in it to last

I haven't been there in too long of a while
In an empirical sense, that is
Frequent visits of my fertile imagination
Have otherwise sated my hunger and thirst
My longing for the dead who were left behind
And all my cravings for the impeccable times
Have been re-lived, time and again, in harmony
Amid the scents of a caring love ever so painstakingly

I borrowed an eagle's eye on this special day
Then perched atop a bastion and began to sway

Palaces, teahouses, trolleys, Bazaars, cafés, fishermen
Rare carpet-Kilim and antiquities-selling ambitious shops
Yachts, stately mosques, the famed Dolmabahçe Sarai
Freighters, speed-boats, Hovercrafts, scenic jogging paths
Do not interest me in the least . . . the eagle's eye is a loan
Of a refined delicacy. I refuse to waste it for the mundane

On the bottom of the Bosphorus, all of a sudden
Underneath a recent undercurrent, oh so sullen!
Amid seagrass . . .

I spotted my brass keychain

this and that

Of four distinctive keys
On it, my elephant carried on

I towed it heroically
Its movable, pretty trunk
Waved at me ecstatically

I guided us all
To the astonishing Sinopian coasts
To my breathtakingly serene flat-sanctuary

But, I found, to my demise
It no longer was there

Only then, did i recall my dream of last year
On the night of the 2nd month's 14th

And . . .

My loaner eye wept

Naren

the other day, i met Anjana Basu
online, in my pursuit of a vision
one i had many eons ago

if my oft' unexplainable
nevertheless, somewhat reliable
constructively imaginative memory
has served me right, that is

at any rate . . .

i sought her out
inquired about her life
even traveled to Allahabad
to see if, at all, her town of birth
to any extent, would resemble mine

i took a connecting flight to London
where she had been schooled

within a couple of hours
i appeared in Kolkata
at her doorstep

a gracious hostess

she invited me in

her home was grandiose
not in an empirical sense, though
oh no! she knew too well what mattered in life

this and that

love and light shone through her, quite loud
but also, from every nook and cranny
of her otherwise-humble abode
she served us tea with milk and honey
it was prepared in a colonialism-free manner
true to her upbringing, true to her mother-culture

she had also generously gathered up
rashly-improvised, store-bought delicacies
(i had, after all, showed up unannounced)
a delicate, modest-in size-tray showed them off

the residues of the plane food
made my fingers think again
they resisted, they did not reach out
with a strong will, in fact,
more stubbornly than
my eyes' appetite
so, i declined
but with my utmost proper
nay-say-gratitude

we talked and talked
actually, she talked and i listened
to her mesmerizing novellas
her *Black Tongue*, the novel for which
she had been awarded the Hawthornden Fellowship
in Scotland, of all the places

she also related to me
her successful endeavors in script-writing
and much more, much more

as for her otherwise-accomplished self
she did not reveal any details to me

had i not done my homework right
there would be no trace of them now
the subject then came to her "Naren"
an epic story-teller-poem at its best
disguised modestly as a free-verse

thus, began Anjana Basu:

The words I have for Naren are purely prose.
Prose. Prose of a chest
A mat of hair against the sun. Sometimes
It's counting the tiles on a floor
Held down. Or a bed field of crumbs
And a dirty foot. Even greying underwear.
Sometimes an evening spent in hatred
Following in one's head the footsteps of a whore
Down some dark lane or a street of crumbling houses.

These are words for Naren.
Perhaps a synonym for rage or hate.
Or even an undefinable word called love
That you could find in rage or hate.
There are other meanings - even other shades
Left out. Footsteps of a child or whore
Or other women deliberately taken
And then the running back to a familiar bed.
I called it lost child.
There were other words too –
Lover, Boyfriend, ex-Husband, boy-husband.
It meant keeping company in an empty room
With haunted corners. With shame
And a telephone wire.
Company against reason or sense
Or the blotting out of a curtain –hiding
From pigeons or from seeking eyes.

this and that

These were words for Naren.
Are still perhaps.
Pretended love made in a mirror,
A shuddering belly and tonsils hurt
The way a face may flush or voice darken
Denying everything but lust or hate, or accidental love.
Naren's words . . .

when this wonder-filled wondrous woman
of a delicate demeanor ceased her voice to be
her tangibly exquisite, enriching, enchanting
exfoliating, purity-extracting human-ness
took her heavy external load right off of her
and her humanity unraveled itself to me to devour
plenty of leftovers joined together in an orderly row

i am already on my way to bring them over to you

Nimi'ipuu

the French
named them "Pierced Nose"
the ignorant happened to find it befitting
such a limiting tag . . . the signaled practice, however
is known not to have been wide-spread among them at all

othering the other "Self"!
what else is new?

rivers have understood them
the lower Snake River
the Clearwater
the Salmon
as have streams and high plateaus
but also, nature's other gifts of abundance
berries, exotic roots, a wide range of big game
to which they would ask for forgiveness
for having had to kill for survival
while the French and the French-alike
continued their Nez Percè-butchery

what other acts of carnage?
piercing noses alive, perhaps

18th century had for horses a discovery in mind
we owe the ancient gift of horse-breeding
to this sizeable North American tribe
their capable hands helped survive and grow
the largest horse herds in the entire continent
remember the distinctively colored Appaloosa?
a most popular breed in today's U.S. of A.

this and that

looking at this tribe's peoples
even if only through robotic eyes
one cannot help but add to this tale:
what was (or what may still be)
their linguistic family?

but before we raise the question above
we had better not forget our manners!

encyclopedias deliver data on "Sahaptin"
yet, they also attribute many a name to this tongue
"Shahaptin" and "Sahaptian", to mention only a few

imagine
if only *we* had their insights before . . .

jumping rope

hand in hand with its clouds above
the mountain sheds its misty blanket
as if to invite me to unashamedly eavesdrop
the chitter-chatter of a flock of little birds
that went astray hours ago into its vast tranquility

i inhale but hesitate to exhale
in my respect for nature's collective silence
even those darling, utterly hyper minions of her
had their calm tucked in quietly under their wings

what on earth was i, who was i
to disturb their precious harmony?

the remainder of last night's snow
begins now to take an earned nap
high above the sky and down below

first, i sit; then, i stand up
next, i want to jump
up onto the horizon
inside the uncovered sky
so that i may soar beyond eternity
in a tightest embrace of my third eye

this and that

our timeline knows

they must be noted

while their desert of vast sand
still chuckled in cheery child-giggles
with their newborns' crisp, scented tickles
but also drained out countless persistent tears
all of which were soaked by parents' eternal fears

wars were aplenty back then . . .

are you with me?
do you see what i see?

on second thought, never mind!
forget about me!

just look
please, take a good look
with your heart's eyes, however
but hold on all along to your conscience
you will then surely heed the desperate call
for a long overdue set of moments of silence
you will then surely hear the gentle embrace
of ancient times, their monumental reconstructions
of that which had been de-constructed mercilessly
by the fatal fancy of the powers-that-be with destructions

oh, the broken spirits' tears!
oh, those souls-burning tears!

wars are too plentiful today . . .

what a journey!

sitting on the balcony
comforted by a sun-warmed chair
being kissed by the generous morning sun
soaking its reflections in the lake's expansive air

this last day of this journey
promises countless others on my path

oh, what a walk this one has already turned out be!

go ahead and sleep!
do not wait up for me!

oh, you trials, tribulations, sorrows, sadness
i am going to make this one worth my while
to make up for each of the past ordeal-rich years

with steadfast trots
i will fly high and float through the sky
i will sing and dance up there and below
i will soar in my own meager but thus far-loudest roar
i will strut my steadiest steps of my own beat
and i will exclude from my word-supply
anything that closely resembles "defeat"

this and that

inventions, discoveries and donations

inventions

too many of us are offended
become demoralized and uneasy
when we are reminded of "the other"
of "its" masteries, in particular
while we keep on indulging
in "its" stellar gifts to "the self"

dissatisfaction
impatience
dejection

blame the aware few!

why stir up history
as it was written
as it is taught
for "the self"
by "the self"?

why pull the brakes ever
of our speeding time-shuttle
to acknowledge "the other" at last
with "its" long-overdue recognition
to thus contemplate our own human blood?

God forbid!

if though, we so did

we just might realize
for a passing moment, at least
how abundantly "the self" benefited
not merely for a few years but for centuries

from "the other" and "its" still-shedding labor-tears

discoveries

> our lives would not have been the same
> had "the other" not invented or discovered
> nor had left intact for the misuse by "the self"
> "its" surname that is bleeding fresh still
> as taken from "its" sweat and blood
> together with all big and little else
> that to this day dons "its" fame

donations

> un-written yet?
>
> yes!
>
> the subject is Sumerians
> of Ancient Mesopotamia
> "the cradle of civilization"
>
> how often do we come across
> the oft-cited term to belong
> to a lobbying cultural entity
> as if it were for it to own?
>
> no surprises there!
>
> "the self" always seems to bear
> the highest octave to raise
> as a result, it gets the entire praise
> our history books bear witness
>
> those writes, however
> suffer from mono-lithic-lens-itis
> to us, thus, goes the honor

this and that

for one among "the self"
or the other self-appointed "self"

as long as it is not
"the other"

by no means!

moreover

we cheer
from the sidelines
turning ourselves into
a music buff of some order

though we know
deep down we know

blame the aware few!

why alter a make-belief
a working bed-time story
with all its esteemed fake-glory

the invention
of Agriculture
intact with its Plow
and System of Irrigation
the Wheel
the Chariot
the Sailboat
the System of Time
the Concept of Astrology
as well as that of Astronomy
the Map
Mathematics
Urbanization

the Cuneiform
the First Form of Writing

yes!
the First Form of Writing!

still
our history books will
a complete absence of it all

Nay! Oh, nay!
they narrate
The Sumerians?
Ancient Mesopotamia?
The Cradle of Civilization?
Nay! No way!

. . .

feel free now
to fill in the blanks
with worthy names
that await their turn
to make the honorable ranks
out of the abyss of ill-will's omission
we must finally give birth
to their past and present gifts of donation
after all, should that not be our mission?

unless of course
we seek our due commission

. . .

blame the aware few!

this and that

the first snow

Alas! the first snow
does not even take notice
of the children's blood

ilk kar

ne çare ilk kar
çocukların kanını
görmüyor bile

der erste schnee

ach! nicht mal auf das kindesblut
achtet der erste schnee

hülya n. yılmaz

no petting zoo

it was a strange encounter
with a first-timer in my backyard

"my" yard?
not in actuality
after all, they were here
long before i settled in
without an ounce of humility

i was unprepared this time

(no fancy camera or a mobile at hand)

thankfully
my eyes were opened wide
and i took the picture of the hawk
in its stately perching-pride
with my enchanted inside

its persistent presence
appeared too close to mine
quite close i'd say
but it was not intimated
not even in the slightest

as for me
i really cannot say
that i was in my brightest
i was . . . hmm
utterly sleepy at best

the few-feet-long-divide
was still a major delight

this and that

unlike "my" other little animals
that come and leave as they ever so please
run or fly away with no warning
at a single wave of my hand
the hawk made itself a secure seat
out of a branch of a barren tree
right at the border of "my" land
amid many others that were dressed
in dainty leaves

it then flew away

close enough to the ground
i guess it was showing off
what it was (and is) capable of

i stayed on for a while longer
too long for a cold late-November-day
i hoped it would return in a heart-beat
to bring along its uniquely-for me-servings
of exciting discoveries ahead

it did not come back

it probably did sense
how much i was taken aback
by its self-introduction of grace

besides . . .

a being like that
cannot be held in a chain
it is, after all, and must thus remain
an admirably free freest a v i a n

so, i turned
to my good old worn-out wind-chime
hanging downward on a hook
i wanted it to create a tune

the wind, however
(contently in a deep nap)
simply refused to play along

i looked around
and saw that i had
(right at my fingertips)
a symphony of an impeccable brand

"my" other wild birds
"my" leaps-happy squirrels
"my" big and small cotton-tails
"my" time-traveler chipmunks
had all gaily gathered
for a spectacular
tap-dance routine
vying for my attention
about to show off once again
their daily acts of loyal affection

this and that

a coincidence?

Guyana Pastoral kept calling me
from a place i dare not describe
i had no knowledge of that tongue
it was dubbed as Guyanese Creole

i still have no knowledge of that tongue
but assume to understand some words in it
it was only the composer i had to know anyway
and i believe i now have sufficiently learned:
David Dabydeen, Guyana's Ambassador-at-Large
an explorer of the Guyanese history
a member of UNESCO's Executive Board
presenter of "The Forgotten Colony"

a mere sand particle in the sea of colonies . . .
but still, i proceeded to uncover more

the owner of the incredible response
to J.M.W. Turner's *Slave Ship*
that painting's depiction of African slaves
being thrown overboard in chains
Dabydeen's ensuing contemplation
over the submerged body of a
forcefully drowned slave
Slave Ship's success
in its melding of fantasy and history
upon the slave's portrayal
his compelling act
of reclaiming and
redeeming of the past
amid the shadows of his taxing insights
his studious eyes as they remain glued on
the horrors of slavery and colonization
under nauseatingly thickening clouds

that carry on the demonic fame
of the long-renowned barbarians of Europe
his authoritatively-sound delivery
of the migrant predicament
in a modern-day interview:

"I'm inclined to think that Britain has heavily depended on
Us for its material and cultural development. The tribe had
An important say and influence in the [British]development.
You can't be a Guyanese without being a Brit and you can't
Be a Brit without being a Guyanese, or a Caribbean."

recognition came along, it indeed came along
for Dabydeen would not leave any of it alone

in sync with his steadfastly extraordinary ways
he helped the British develop beyond themselves
for he wanted the cast over the bloodied pools
under endless blood-soaked beds no more
he helped the world develop beyond itself
hence, he co-edited a monumental how-to-book
for the walking dead of colonialist barbarisms-at-large
The Oxford Companion to Black British History
"a magisterial excavation of Black Britain"

one award after another raced to the doors of Dabydeen
for his editing work but also to record his poetic worth

the winner of the Commonwealth Poetry Prize
a masterful novelist
a model scholar
a literary-icon-educator
Director of the Centre for Caribbean Studies
Professor at the Centre for
British Comparative Cultural Studies
at the University of Warwick
and much much more . . .

this and that

a coincidence?

i think not!

my modest discovery
of the Highly Esteemed
David Dabydeen
was simply meant to be

for it has materialized
at a time of an utterly-trying
professional hardship of mine
(not to exclude any contemplation
on poetry's meaning to me)
a hole-filled life-ring in a turbulent sea
with a nearby-view of the long-lost years
to no longer be, David rescued me

a professor, passionate in teaching
a heavily-faded scholar of some past merit
a self-oppressed struggling writer of fiction
a poet, starving for self-love with much to tell
including the 'migrant condition'
though not of Black History alone
nor purely of David's "Slave Song"

i wouldn't know though
where and how to begin
in my effort to avoid risking
a disservice to any recognized
noteworthy gem in the field
such initiative is, after all, not,
cannot nor will ever be mine to claim

so, it is my own path that i follow
but there is a significant sorrow
which i dare to pierce through
at least with one faint shadow

i shall choose to courageously move on
whenever wherever the ground is apt

of course, always, in all ways
with fiery thanks from the soul
to that spellbindingly affluent tongue
called ever-so-modestly the Guyanese Creole

this and that

where are you now?

i miss the untainted i inside you
you caressed my birth into your bosom
on you, i laid down my many beloveds

my mother's unforgettable touch
my father's sacrificial feel
my uncles' pain-soothing embraces
my granddaddy's gentlest laughter
my Yasemin's exceptional beauty
are for me no more
you have taken them all
as for my brother, whom i
utterly adore, i live no more

you have changed from the core

so many famed traversed through your terrains
they left their bountiful legacy with you
i now understand as to why
Nâzım Hikmet would oft' cry
in his prison cell for too long of a while
even your by him-envied-age-old landscape
of his countless sleepless nights' saving grace
is recognizable no more

you have changed from the core

today, i feel
as if i grew up
in a fairy tale

hülya n. yılmaz

"Once upon a time"
you were to me
a mesmerizing spell
everything in-between
had also its magical charm
"And they lived happily ever after"
however, oh, my sweet Turkey
has been nothing but a pathetic lie

i still cannot help but find myself to be
in a desperate chase after your unrivaled lore
i seem to be unable to restrain the primordial urge
to honor your enlightened past and its memories of me
although you have most certainly changed from the core

this and that

in search of . . .

a few meaningful lines
all along while Clio whines
Calliope is nowhere to be seen
as for Erato Melpomene and Polyhymnia
they are getting dressed right before my eyes
in a frantic vengeance and joy i have not foreseen

all i had requested were a few leads
to embark on my quest to find the Lupita
i suspect, i am suffering from severe jitters
as i am capable of only counting my fingers
while each compiles in a pile many a countless bead

i'm afraid, i am going to drown in this Chlorophyta

perhaps, just perhaps though
i will find what i think i am looking for
would you, please, bear with me while i search
until a reasonably coherent finding does emerge?

Eureka!

i did find it!
i finally did!
i, indeed, found an encyclopedia
ever so proud of its voluminous bit
"Britannica", its makers unanimously call it

i can never keep on a pedestal any colonialist . . .

my jottings clearly announce thus, don't you think?

as for my effort to rise as a weighty conversationalist
i truly hold not even one single hope for your "Hallelujah!"
but would you, please, join me at least
in my jump to an eager "Hurrah"?
i am, after all, finishing up the task at hand . . . no easy feat
otherwise, i would have to throw a never-before-seen-fit

this and that

Pachacuti

an Inca Emperor takes the throne
"Pachacuti" is his name
his rule becomes a legacy
and attains a sizeable fame
for its unrivaled magnitude
as South America's rarity

modern cultural history
traces the Inca to the 12th century

AD, that is
in the Andes of southeastern Peru

if one were to look
from a frozen space in a distance . . .

Manco Capac, the son of the
Inca's supposed creator, was
journeyed by his father
the Sun God Inti
down to Earth

12 million people of a large diversity
comprising 100 different sets of ethnicities
made up Tawantinsuyu, the Inca state
thus, claim the sources of histories

using their intellect effectively
helped them survive
a vast amount of misery

they were helpless, however
in the face of the worst kind of agony
people in power had waited long enough

time had already passed by too fast
and had traveled away, way too far
for them to establish methodically
an all-inclusive unbeatable tyranny

there is much more to narrate about the Inca
a huge number of encyclopedias is on e-call
what matters to me though lies beneath the shell
that which i will unearth with vigor, oh yes, i shall
in fact, it is nothing new that i choose to seek
to dare to unbury discoveries is not for the meek
so, let us go on to play our convenient hide-and-seek

powers-to-be?

today?

no way!

be that as it may
some of us are here to stay
and will turn over stones for sure
to unravel the treasures of this mystery
then, powers-to-be will be no more

have no dismay!

if . . .

if you indeed shine in life
as if nothing else but love matters
your final breath will last forever
and it will not let in even one single taint
for your primeval light of love
will never adapt to a color of faint

Eğer ki . . .

Eğer ki ışıdıysan hayatta içten
sevgi dışında hiçbir anlam yokmuşçasına
ebedi kalır en son nefesin
özünü yitirmemesine
çünkü asıl aşk ışığın
asla bırakmaz kendini ölüme

wenn . . .

wenn auch du so scheinst im leben
als gelte ausser liebe nichts
bleibt ewig dein atem-ende
ohne sich zu verderben
denn dein erstes licht der liebe
lässt sich nie versterben

hülya n. yılmaz

A Special Place

hülya n. yılmaz

lost . . . or?

people
in every corner of the fountain-square
some seating is available close-by
we walk toward one left-out spot
and sit down in our wonderous awe
under the watchful faces' curious eyes
accompanied by what i assume to be
a traditional Moroccan drum tune
mesmerizing the clear night-sky
competing with the vibrant Arabic sounds
that rise higher and higher up
from countless chats
of those for us-undecodable voices

i want to dance to the enticing rhythm
but i know this place is not mine to claim . . .

many families are promenading
with their older children
minding the safe navigations
of their little ones' toddler-go-carts
those beautiful small darlings
are grinning from ear to ear
overjoyed with their driving skills
while they keep an eye on the passers-by
their age-alike counterparts, that is
who travel around the plaza
donning many different car models
of a variety of colors and sizes
in that enviable-even-by adults
modern day-invention

hülya n. yılmaz

one blond boy
about 2 years old
discovers the fun of obstacle-jumping
he steps his cute little feet atop a brick
among many that shelter a healthy tree
he jumps down from it
onto the plaza's floor-concrete
while his parents talk eagerly on a bench

no boo boos
none whatsoever
he is so elated by his daring stunt
that he repeats the same in reverse
tummy-laughing in audible giggles

young couples also pass by
some glance at us in subdued demeanors
others stare bluntly and persistently
we smile and mind our own business

there are many boys of different ages
they play all kinds of outdoor games
with their fathers or with each other
girls strut their perhaps-newly-learned
steps of awakening-femininity
they look left, then right, then left again
assessing on a scale of their own making
the attention they get from the opposite sex

a round ball seems to be
the biggest attraction for some of the boys
several of them don complete soccer uniforms
with barely-worn out shoes to match
others among their team members

stand out with their everyday clothes
they make a serious effort
to keep their bathroom slippers in place

one older boy
joins the game with overt enthusiasm
he is wearing a traditional male Hijab
quite a talent this young man is
with all his rapid feet-moves and leg twists
despite his neck-to-ankle-length-garb

nearest to our seats
two women-groups gather up
they sit in opposite ends
from one another
but their focus of interest
appears to be the same: gossip
their mimics and gestures are universal
descriptions of female bodies and faces
via finger-and-face-adjustments
along with the uniquely fiery octaves
of their voices, which yield to
a large variety of enunciations
flavored with laughter as well as snorts
a sign-language of disapproval? aplenty!

the same drum-tune enters the open-air again
the performers' break must be over

i want to dance to the enticing rhythm
but i know this place is not mine to claim . . .

yet, i am made to feel as if it were

hülya n. yılmaz

wherever i went and stayed this summer
a sense of belonging has been gifted to me
in Bethlehem
Ramallah
Amman
Madaba
Jericho
Cairo
Giza
Kenitra
Larache
Assilah
Monastir
Rahovec
Prizren
Skopje
Strumica

    i was embraced by the ultimate warmth of loving hearts
       all the dearest souls in these parts of the globe
         have abundantly demonstrated to me
          as to why their acts of hospitality
           oozing from their hometowns
          and cultural entities at large
            have long ago attained
             their worldwide fame

Epilogue

about hülya n. yılmaz

A retired Liberal Arts Penn State professor, hülya n. yılmaz [sic] is Co-Chair and Director of Editing Services at Inner Child Press International. She is a long-time member of both, the Academy of American Poets and the Editorial Freelancers Association.

After earning her doctoral degree from The University of Michigan, hülya has settled in North America. Her service for academia spans over forty years during which she has designed and taught special-topic courses involving comparative literature subject matters, including women's literature and film within the Islamic context, non-western feminisms, literary reflections on cross-cultural influences in prominent West-European entities, Sufism –the mystical tradition of Islam and the impact of Rumi's Sufi poetry on the 19th and 20th century German literature. In addition to her numerous presentations at national and international conferences, she has authored *Das Ghasel des islamischen Orients in der deutschen Dichtung / The Ghazal of the Muslim Orient in German* Literature, which is an extensive book of scholarly research on the literary influence of the Muslim East upon western Europe with a concentrated focus on Germany between the 19th and 21st centuries. Her analysis of *Snow*, the 2006 Nobel Prize of Literature recipient Orhan Pamuk's "only political novel" (per Pamuk's own words in an interview) through the work's examination under the lenses of Sufism has as an invited book chapter, "The Imagined Exile: Orhan Pamuk in His Novel *Snow*" in *Global Perspectives on Orhan Pamuk* (pp. 109-124), published by Palgrave Macmillan US in 2012.

hülya has authored *Trance*, a tri-lingual book of poetry along with her own translations, and *Aflame. Memoirs in Verse*, and co-authored *An Aegean Breeze of Peace.* Like her writings, also her English-German-Turkish literary translations epitomize her two sources of creative thirst – teaching and writing. Now in its 6th year, *The Year of the Poet* is an international anthology to which hülya contributes every month with her poems, some of which she has presented at poetry events in- and outside the U.S., including Kosovo, Canada, Jordan and Tunisia. Her poetry has been published in an excess of sixty-two anthologies of global endeavors, and as of April 15, 2017, two of her poems remain recorded in a U.S.-wide poetry exhibition, *Telepoem Booth* – a permanent public art installation. On May 25, 2018, the Writers International Network of British Colombia, Canada (WIN) honored hülya with a poetry award. Her short prose, including feature articles, professional prefaces, introductions, forewords and epilogues, has appeared in literary publications of national and international makeup.

The author is currently working on four book-length literary manuscripts: two poetry collections in Turkish and English with her own English translations, *Toruncanlarıma, for My Grandchildren* and *homeland*; a collection of poems in English, *a female in the third space* and a collection of short stories, *Once upon a Time in Turkey . . . hülya's Turkish tales*.

yılmaz finds it vital for everyone to understand a deeper sense of self and writes creatively to attain a comprehensive awareness for and development of our humanity.

What Others Are Saying...

Hülya N. Yılmaz engages us with storytelling that compels our attention. She walks us through life's paces with that edge of understanding that draws us into the writing and makes us turn the page for more.

Her opening poem, "i still breathe", sets the tone for this work as she says, "in the silence of the night / i breathe / devouring everything the universe serves me". This is a taste of what is to come.

Her poem, "not a mere train ride", is telling in the verse, "life suddenly had no taste no meaning anymore". She weaves a hard but tender story of loss and pain that comes to the surface of memories of her Mom boarding a train to go to a best friend. The hint of loss that goes deeper than her Dad's explanation makes us wonder.

After strolling landscapes with Hülya, you will say yes, this is storytelling that makes us take notes.

Teresa E. Gallion
New Mexico, US

Poet
Author of *Contemplation in the High Desert*, Chasing *Light* and *On the Wings of the Wind* (CD)
www.teresagallion.yolasite.com

Hülya's collection of poems in her book, *this and that* is the celebration of disparate yet harmonious thoughts and ideas that pass through our mind all the time. It's a deliberate and measured blending of emotions, sentiments and feelings. She uses heart, mind and soul as colorful threads to knit a beautiful quilt to shield us from cold negativity. The power of her love can be experienced by anyone prepared to wrap her verses in an embrace.

Each poem is a small universe in which the poet creates multi-dimensional life within each facet of her life. With a wide diversity of themes there is something for everyone in this charming yet compelling - a must read book.

Ashok K Bhargava
Vancouver, British Columbia

Poet
Author of *Riding Alone* and *Riding the Tide*
President,
Writers International Network Canada
at Government of British Columbia
http://writersinternationalnetwork.wordpress.com
http://ashokbhargava.wordpress.com

Having been given the privilege to read the new, masterfully written book of poetry by the esteemed professor, Dr. Hülya N. Yılmaz, *this and that* before its publication, I am in a position to humbly comment-, with a dose of healthy envy- that her unparalleled poems:

> Warm the heart
> Inspire the mind
> Uplift the spirit and
> Soar the soul to the heights of poetic bliss!

From the depths of my heart, I wish Dr. Yılmaz that her book sales over the ocean of success, unimpeded, so as to reach the harbor of world-recognition that it truly and rightfully deserves.

Demetrios Trifiatis
Athens, Greece

Poet
Professor of Philosophy, Ph.D.
Author of *Lessons Life Taught Me* and Co-Author of *An Aegean Breeze of Peace*

Creative people come up with something innovative that has a profound impact and leaves behind a distinctive mark – it may be a rare word changing the commonly misconstrued concepts and developing meaning in an upscale fashion; it may be an artistic initiative seeking a renaissance in human thought, and thus, transferring it to a higher level of distributing knowledge.

An ordinary person, but one who sees things from an extraordinary perspective and delivers them in her own unique way to a higher path of understanding, leaves an unusual impression with her work; thus, leads the recipients to acceptance.

Love and peace serve creations when these sentiments are authentic and devoted to the truth of their ethics and to an interaction with others, indifferent to the conceived notions about differences concerning race, religion, and ideological affiliation.

Our respected poet is respectful. Her writings first ask to be read and then, to be accepted. Her affiliation to humanity mirrors a law that calls for love, brotherhood, cooperation and co-existence. Her style is leveled and easy to understand.

As a poet seeking to awaken the person from his intellectual slumber and plant love, kindness and humanitarian roots in the soul in order to flourish the fruits of nature and encourage to live side by side without the presence of artificially created divisions, such as racism or other ideologies. A poet is capable of raising in the reader awareness for the forced divides as far as humanity and has, thus, the potential to move in him / her pure human emotions.

What surfaces in *this and that* is the evidence of a strong personality characteristic. This trait of Hülya N. Yılmaz is what touched me as far as my physical reality when destiny gave our families the chance to meet in person; when we gathered in brotherly love, broke bread together and communed over many different points of interest and matters of life. Congratulations to you for this book, oh moral child, oh noble and gentle child!

This book is an invitation to restore the losses that wars and other violent conflicts between people inflict on humanity, moving it away from the bonds of love and solidarity. The poetic voice of Hülya N. Yılmaz penetrates into our sense of humanity, seeking to establish a universal discourse that brings us together. In that togetherness, we are given the rare opportunity to measure our ability in elevating ourselves above our differences, all of which are forced upon us – differences that have etched into our history wars and other bloody conflicts, differences that prevent us from raising us to a world of peace and love. The words of the poet in this case invite the intellectual to assume responsibility for the enlightening of the minds and to become the leaders of a secure future in which we all can build a common dream that brings us back to the moment of our original beginning – the moment of reconciliation and satisfaction with ourselves, our sense of humanity and our love. This book actually glows deep love, as it introduces a language through which love becomes our faith.

Aziz Mountassir Aziz Mountassir
Larache, Morocco

Poet
Professor at Ministère De L'éducation National
Cultural Ambassador (Morocco) at
Inner Child Press International
Author of *Double Play and Pain*, *Scratches on the Waiting Face*, *As Much as Fancy Comes Reproaching* and *Silence Addresses Abandonment*

Hülya N. Yılmaz' *"this and that"* . . .

Tihomir Jancovski
Skopje, Macedonia

Poet, Translator and Columnist
Author of *The Noise of Loneliness* (poetry), *Straight Forward* (poetry), *Two Worlds, Rumi* (poetry translation), Mother Tongue and Other Poems, Ahmed Buric (poetry translation), *Lydia, or All I Know About Women* (novel), *Conditioned Freedom* (Bosnian poetry anthology, translation), *153 Chapters on Prayer, Evagrius Ponticus* (spiritual manual, translation), *A Hat for my Head* (short stories and columns collection) and *Of Late* (poetry)

Realizing that there is no East and West but the world is a sphere that absorbs the Plethora yet keeping its splendor and beauty as a jewel in the crown of Eternity, Yılmaz is a progeny of the quintessence of Creation: As an individual who is modest beyond the human perception and as a woman in her all-embracing maternal valor to remain what she originally was since the time when Souls were created to the NOW and the Hereafter. As a poet (I shall get back to this later), she is a Lava of the blue color of Love that warms and soothes, that returns to its primordial essence.

There are two permissions I would ask for, if I may be granted to adore someone outside Almighty in this world: Woman and Poetry. The dilemma still remains which one to adore first; or, shall I reverently uplift both to the level of Eternal Light in the weft of Creation, as one single Soul – sparkling, bedazzling, luminous, and only as such, able to emit the rainbow color of Creation. Indeed, my words do not have an end. So, I ask readers not to catch them but to read them just as they are: Not a metaphor, a hyper-valuation, or God forbid, an intoxication with the persona and Poet Hülya N. Yılmaz. The truth is that whatever I say it is and will always be only a particle in the Abyss of Surface, whereas Yılmaz's totality is far richer and far more complementary than one may truly realize.

She diminishes another dilemma – that of the Scholar and that of the Artist, both of which she "Elfishly" braids into a unique oneness, and she does so only with the impulse of her Creativity.

Her poetry emits experience, that of her life's journey, with an awareness of the Sufi doctrine of Divine Love, the beauty of nature and creation, the beauty of the human soul, the struggles, the longings and of heritage and inheritance – all coiled in a bobbin of Poetry with such an amazing skill and sublime craftsmanship. A real word master, the only one who is able to hand over her dowry to the upcoming generation of writers.

To preserve my own delight and that of her readers, I would not spoil any of her lines in quoting her verses because I want to let the reader solely absorb the veracity of my above-mentioned words.

Thank you, Dr. Yılmaz.

Thank you, Poet Hülya N. Yılmaz for giving me a chance so that I, bare-foot, may enter your abode of creativity and immense knowledge.

Fahredin Shehu
19.12.2018
Prishtina, Kosova

Poet, Philosopher, Essayist
Director and Organizer, International Poetry Festival in Kosovo (1ˢᵗ in 2015)
Author of *Nun*, *Invisible Plurality*, *Nektarina*, *Elemental 99*, *Kun*, *Dismantle of Hate*, *Crystalline Echoes*, *Pleroma's Dew*, *Emerald Macadam*, *Maelstrom*, *Neon Child* and **HERENOW**

Hülya N. Yılmaz' poetic reflections, have a descriptive sensitivity, in a most creative and captivating manner.

I find reading her an experience of having an encounter with, to coin a phrase, a poetic conversationalist, who wants to make you feel part of our world's condition, as she poetically describes. Be that of a somewhat personal level, or thus of man's ever alarming disruptive preside. Either way, she does so ever convincingly. Hülya N. Yılmaz is indeed a poet to be read!

Jean-Jacques Fournier
Montreal, Canada

Poet
Author of *Issues ~ of black and white ~* (2nd edition), *Matters ~ of body and soul ~* (2nd edition), *Images ~ in shades and shadows ~* (2nd edition), *Places ~ of loss and found ~, Obliquities ~ of a lucid mind ~, Reflexions ~ of a probing eye ~, Kaleidoscope ~ musings of life chronicles ~, A Hyphenated World ~ held fitting guise ~, A Scent of Reality ~ be inherent perception ~, Held Instant ~ on life's clock ~, Conjugated People ~ by shade ~* and *Chaos ~ a human side of man ~*

I am honoured to be one of the reviewers of Professor Hülya N. Yılmaz' new book offering, *this and that*.

this and that is an evocative, poignant, and creative collection of eclectic pieces as well as enriching reads of Professor Yılmaz' signature writing style. Each piece evokes different feelings, and readers can very much relate to them.

My favourite poems in the book are, "i still breathe" and "Daddy." The first one is an interesting and soulful composition which leaves one breathless. "In the silence of the night / i breathe / and i devour everything the universe serves me [. . .]" My second favourite is close to my heart since it is about a "Daddy." I thought about my own late Dad in her poem and I found it so beautiful and melodramatic: "how many times have I imagined myself / holding that spoon and that soup-bowl [. . ."

this and that is yet another wonderful gift of Professor Yılmaz to readers and lovers of words and poetry and will surely touch people's hearts. She never fails to engage her readers through her rhythmic, dancing words, and I do highly recommend this book not just to poetry enthusiasts but to lovers of literature as well.

My warm congratulations again to Professor Hülya N. Yılmaz for another amazing and beautiful book!

Elizabeth Esguerra Castillo
Antipolo, Philippines

Poet, Feature Writer, Journalist, English Instructor
Author of *Inner Reflections of the Muse*

HÜLYA YILMAZ' *this and that* ~ In Turkish

Dil şairin evidir. Hülya Yılmaz'ın üç evi var. Kendini rahat hissettiği, kültürünü taşıdığı, tanıştığı üç dil. Üç dille yazıyor Hülya Yılmaz. Dilin mekanla da ilgisi var elbet. Yaşadığı yer, mesafe, hayatın getirdiği mecburiyetler. Bunu en çok "Daddy" şiirinde hissediyoruz. Şiir iki dilde kaleme alınmış ve iki dilde de etkisini yitirmiyor. Kökler ve uzaklaşan mekanları hissettiren önemli bir şiir. Diğer şiirlerinde de bu çok dilli anlatımı görüyoruz. Özellikle bölüm geçişlerinde gördüğümüz, haiku'ları andıran şiirler üç dilde yazılmış. Hülya Yılmaz'ın şiirleri sadece dil açısından zengin değil aynı zamanda biçim açısından da zengin. Yeni anlatım şekillerini deneyen bir şair kendisi. Yeni şekil yeni anlamlar taşır şiirde. Bunu net bir şekilde görüyoruz Hülya Yılmaz'ın şiirinde.

Hülya Yılmaz yaşadığını yazan bir şair. Şiirindeki güç buradan geliyor kanımca. Somut olaylarda, mekanlarda görüyoruz onun şiirini. Doğaya bakıyor ve oradan konuşuyor. Kimi zaman sincaplarla sohbet eder, kimi zaman rüzgar onu öper. Bazen bir kelebek ziyarete gelir, bazen de yapraklar yağmur olur. Kar, yağmur, ağaç, kuşlar, böcekler hepsi bir yandan akıyor şiirlerde.

Bir ayağı hep dışarıda bir şair Hülya Yılmaz. Akdeniz'den Inca'lara, Sümerler'den İstanbula, Ma'rib'ten Ürdün'e, Mısır'dan Ankara'ya geniş bir coğrafyadan sesleniyor. Hepsinin kültürüne, doğasına, insanına dokunan bir şair. Çocuklarının acısını hatırlatan, insanlarına ses olan bir şair. İnce duyguları olan, hassas bir şair.

Şafak Çelik
Istanbul, Turkey

Poet, Story-Writer, Essayist
Author of *İlk Değilim Üstelik* and *Kuş Adımı*
http://safakcelik.com/

HÜLYA YILMAZ' *this and that* ~ In Translation

Language is the home of a poet. Hülya Yılmaz has three homes. Three languages through which she feels comfortable and transliterates her culture and with which she is thoroughly familiar. Hülya Yılmaz writes in three languages.

Language, of course, is also related to space. Where the poet lives, distances, the necessities life brings along . . . We sense these in her poem, "Daddy" in particular. This piece is written in two languages and it does not lose its impact in either version. This is an important poem that enables the reader to feel one's roots and the spaces left behind in a distant past. We see this multi-lingual composition also in her other poems. Her poems constructed in HAIKU-like forms in the transitional sections of her book, in particular, are written in three languages.

Hülya Yılmaz' poems are rich not only in her choice of the language but are also rich constructs as far as form. She is a poet who experiments with innovative styles of narration. New forms assume new meaning in poetry; or better yet, they lend new meaning to a poetic work. This phenomenon is succinctly evident in Hülya Yılmaz' poetry.

Hülya Yılmaz is a poet who writes what she lives. Therein lies the strength of her poetry. We find her poems in actual occurrences and spaces. She observes nature and speaks from that position. At times, she communicates with squirrels and at other times, the wind kisses her. Sometimes, a butterfly comes for a visit with her; sometimes, falling leaves become the rain. The snow, the rain, trees, birds, insects, all pour over her poems together.

Hülya Yılmaz is a poet with one foot always outside her physical space. Her voice carries the scent of a vast number of places and peoples. She speaks with us, to us within an expansive system of geography; from the Mediterrenean to the Incas, from the Sumerians to İstanbul, from Ma'rib to Jordan, from Egypt to Ankara. She is one such poet who, while conveying her observations and experiences to the reader, reaches out with a sincere touch to all the cultures, together with their natural environments and peoples, she writes about. She is one such poet who reminds us of the suffering of their children and lends a voice to their human condition – a poet of heightened sensitivity regarding humanity at large, a poet of refined emotions.

Translated by hülya yılmaz
With the permission and approval of **Şafak Çelik**

Reading through hülya n. yılmaz's *this and that*, one begins with the restless feeling of "i continue to call though in fact it is not so at all: the human species" ("i still breathe"), becomes one with her dear father's "Hüliş" as she reminisces about him ("Daddy" and "oh, my sweet Daddy!"), flies with a bird "strategically / dropping the seeds to the ground / another bird of the same kind cautiously perched / on the now-delicatessen-filled lawn below / waiting to be fed" ("a yet-unborn poem"), feel love and gratitude "for all that everything we were for each other once. Be well, dear heart! Be very well! Always and forevermore" ("Ahh, that Mediterranean Breeze!"), travels with her through the globe with a sense of "wherever i went and stayed this summer / a sense of belonging has been gifted to me" ("lost . . . or?") and find insightful answers in her "is that what we call ours, ours?" For me personally, reading through hülya n. yılmaz's poetry collection, *this and that*, has been a journey of self-discovery with a deep admiration for her keen observations of human nature, her own personal experiences of life and living and above all, her concern for humanity! hülya's *this and that* is about all these and a lot more, written in her simple and lucid yet subtle style that tugs at one's heartstrings – an unputdownable must-read!!!

Padmaja Iyengar-Paddy
Hyderabad, India
Writer, Poet, Editor & Reviewer

This and That . . .

I am often enraptured by a voice in another experience . . . throughout *this and that*, I have the opportunity to close my eyes to hear some of this and some of that. The very preface of "in the tongue of another" allows to me to be whisked away to the story, the recalling and the life of Hülya. It is not often that a writer will secret you in their pocket so that you can bear witness to the life of another. Hülya not only allows space in her pocket but also prepares a place for you to ride comfortably.

I have often thought that a translation should bear more in mind of the intention of the translation that that of the what we often feel needs translating. What I have learned is to live with "hope-eyes" and to see what is offered. "[W]hat i thought i knew would simply not do", or so I am told on page 58. When did we learn to see concrete instead of cities, leaves instead of trees?

As children we speak as we see it, we learn as we need to, and no one corrects that experience. Hülya's *this and that* is life as we live it. Thank you Hülya, for this exceptional gift of you.

Gail Weston Shazor
Charlotte Amalie, U.S. Virgin Islands

Poet

Author of *an Overstanding of an Imperfect Love, notes from the Blue Roof, Lies My Grandfathers Told me* and featured songs in ReverbNation
innerchildpressanthologies@gmail.com

In her book, *this and that* Hülya Yılmaz combines different topics, inspired by personal life situations, moments or certain experiences. The unfolding of evocation is so deep that it captures you in the magic of her poetic world.

Different life charms, but sensitive moments also, like missing a lost father, human nature, trials, successes and failing in realizations of human goals and realization of the task, also the dreams of every individual which leave marks to this world, compose a powerful mosaic in verse that urges you to explore this rich treasure in this collection. Mastering the beauty of the various elements, in a rich poetic language, shows the poet's creative experience. Therefore, her poetry, in *this and that* swallows you in a world of beauty inside a verse. This makes Yılmaz a poet who every reader can find themselves in her work.

Besa Hoxha Beqiri
Prishtina, Kosovo

Poet
Ph.D. in Literature
Professor at AAB University

hülya's

Other Books

An Aegean Breeze of Peace

by

Demetrios Trifiatis

and

hülya n. yılmaz

a few words from the ublisher . . .

Needless to say, for a vast variety of endearing reasons, I am impartial to the character, the spirit, and the personage of our dear hülya n. yılmaz. I have had a ringside seat since 2013 which afforded me to observe her magnificent evolution.

When I consider hülya's poetry, I myself am intrigued by her delicate means of telling stories within her verse as she shares the intimacies of her consciousness of her past as well as that which she experiences in her now. She has a unique voice that emotes from within her magical core that is able to not only capture, but to transcribe the moments that move her and relate them to her readers in such a way that it feels like you are looking through the eyes of her soul. I could go on with the many accolades of wonder, but that would perhaps serve to water down the wonder to be found in her words, which will minimize the effect of self-discovery as you read on.

In parting, let me say this . . . as a poet myself, the most profound aspect I feel that needs to be conveyed is our voice of authenticity. This relates to not only our experiences, but our imaginations and all the other little life-nuances that inspire us to speak. I am thankful in so many ways for the voice of our dear hülya, for it allows one to not only escape the mundane, but additionally empowers us, the readers to believe in the magic . . . each in our own way. Thank You, dear hülya for being who you are.

William S. Peters, Sr.

Pulitzer Nominee Poet
Author of an excess of fifty books of poetry

Inner Child Press

Inner Child Press is a publishing company founded and operated by writers. Our personal publishing experiences provide us an intimate understanding of the sometimes-daunting challenges writers, new and seasoned may face in the business of publishing and marketing their creative "Written Work".

For more information
Inner Child Press

www.innerchildpress.com

intouch@innerchildpress.com

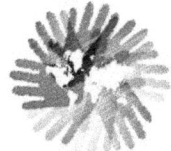

Inner Child Press International
'building bridges of cultural understanding'
202 Wiltree Court, State College, Pennsylvania 16801

www.innerchildpress.com

www.ingramcontent.com/pod-product-compliance
Lightning Source LLC
Chambersburg PA
CBHW021002090426
42738CB00007B/625